Garfield eats his heart out

BY: JIM DAVIS

BALLANTINE BOOKS · NEW YORK

All rights reserved under International and Pan-American Copyright Conventions. Published in the United States by Ballantine Books, a division of Random House, Inc., New York, and simultaneously in Canada by Random House of Canada Limited, Toronto, Canada.

Library of Congress Catalog Card Number: 82-90830
ISBN: 0-345-32018-2

Manufactured in the United States of America

First Edition: March 1983

30

GARFIELD DIET TIPS

1. Never go back for seconds—get it all the first time.

2. Set your scales back five pounds.

3. Never accept a candygram.

4. Don't date Sara Lee.

5. Vegetables are a must on a diet. I suggest carrot cake, zucchini bread and pumpkin pie.

6. Never start a diet cold turkey (maybe cold roast beef, cold lasagna…).

7. Try to cut back. Leave the cherry off your ice cream sundae.

8. Hang around people fatter than you.

FETCH, BOY

JIM DAVIS

6-8

OBEDIENT...
NOT VERY BRIGHT,
BUT OBEDIENT

6-9

JIM DAVIS

OH, GARFIELD

PUNT!

© 1981 United Feature Syndicate, Inc

BOING! BOING! BOING! BOING!

CRASH!

JIM DAVIS

I LOVE YOU WHEN YOU'RE NAUGHTY

6-14

I'M BORED

6-21

BORED, BORED, BORED

THERE MUST BE MORE THINGS TO DO ON A SCREEN DOOR THAN JUST HANG HERE

JIM DAVIS

© 1981 United Feature Syndicate, Inc.

NICE GOING, DUMMY

6-28

JIM DAVIS

© 1981 United Feature Syndicate, Inc.

WAHCHOO!

SNIFF

Dear Garfield,
How do I avoid the embarrassment of cat hairs all over my house when I have company?
Harried

SIMPLE

NEVER INVITE ANYONE TO YOUR HOME AGAIN

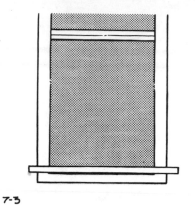

FISH STORE

7-5

FISH STORE

JIM DAVIS

FISH STORE

OH YUK!

WHAT DID YOU DRAG THAT FISH IN FOR?

SMACK!

BONK!

WHEN A CAT PRESENTS YOU WITH A DEAD, SMELLY THING, IT'S AN EXPRESSION OF LOVE, YOU TWIT

© 1981 United Feature Syndicate. Inc.

HERE'S A LESSON IN THE NATURAL ORDER OF THINGS

JIM DAVIS

CATS USE CLAWS TO CLIMB TREES

AND FIRE DEPARTMENTS TO GET DOWN

7-6 © 1981 United Feature Syndicate, Inc.

WHAT DOES GARFIELD THE CAT DO WHEN HE'S STUCK UP A TREE?

JIM DAVIS   7-7

WHY WHAT ANY HONORABLE CAT WOULD DO, OF COURSE

WAHHH!

© 1981 United Feature Syndicate, Inc.

I'M GETTING OUT OF THIS TREE

7-8

JIM DAVIS

BOING!

I DIDN'T ALLOW FOR MY RESILIENT NATURE

© 1981 United Feature Syndicate, Inc.

POOR ME... STUCK UP A TREE

JIM DAVIS

7-9

THINGS COULD BE WORSE, I GUESS

© 1981 United Feature Syndicate, Inc.

7-13

7-14

LET ME GIVE YOU A DRIVING LESSON, GARFIELD

WHEN YOU'RE AS GOOD A DRIVER AS I AM, YOU DRIVE DEFENSIVELY

7-19

YOU LOOK BOTH WAYS AT AN INTERSECTION

JIM DAVIS

© 1981 United Feature Syndicate, Inc.

THEN YOU PROCEED WITH CAUTION

HONK! SCREEEE!

DARN YOU, GARFIELD

I'M SUCH A KIDDER

YOU KNOW IT'S MONDAY WHEN YOU FIND SHARKS CIRCLING IN YOUR WATER BOWL

GARFIELD

© 1981 United Feature Syndicate, Inc. 8-3

I'M IN THE MOOD FOR A GOOD FIGHT, BUT I AM PERSONALLY OPPOSED TO SENSELESS VIOLENCE

PUNT!

THAT'S FOR NOT BEING A CAT

8-4 © 1981 United Feature Syndicate, Inc.

WHAT DO YOU WANT TO DO TONIGHT, GARFIELD? DO YOU WANT TO GO JOGGING? GO TO A MOVIE? PLAY MINIATURE GOLF

8-7

JIM DAVIS

OR WOULD YOU RATHER GO EAT?

NATCH

© 1981 United Feature Syndicate, Inc.

DO YOU TAKE YOUR CAT EVERYWHERE?

8-8

JIM DAVIS

YES, WE DO EVERYTHING TOGETHER, MY DEAR

EXCEPT MAKE PASSES AT UGLY WAITRESSES

© 1981 United Feature Syndicate, Inc.

PAT
PAT
PAT

JiM DAViS

POOMP!

I WOULD HAVE
HAD TO EAT HIM
TO SAVE FACE

8-16

HEY, GARFIELD, GUESS WHAT?

THE DOG NEXT DOOR IS BEING GIVEN A BIRTHDAY PARTY TODAY

THIS BRICK SHOULD MAKE A SPIFFY GIFT

© 1981 United Feature Syndicate, Inc.

BONK
YIP!

YIP!

HAPPY BIRTHDAY, DOG

8-23

HELLO, DOCTOR? DO YOU THINK YOU COULD SURGICALLY REMOVE MY CAT FROM A DOG

JIM DAVIS

IMAGINE ME DOING A CAT FOOD COMMERCIAL

8-26 JIM DAVIS

NEXT THERE'LL BE THE MOVIE OFFERS, THE SCREAMING FANS, THE LIMOUSINES...

BELLY, YOU AND I ARE GOING PLACES

© 1981 United Feature Syndicate, Inc.

IS THIS WHERE MY CAT AUDITIONS FOR THE CAT FOOD COMMERCIAL?

YEH

8-27 JIM DAVIS

HEY, LARRY. BREAK OUT THE WIDE-ANGLE LENS

IF I DON'T GET THE PART, THE DIRECTOR IS GOING TO BE SPORTING THOSE SHADES UP HIS RIGHT NOSTRIL

© 1981 United Feature Syndicate, Inc.

I CAN'T REACH THAT PIE, NERMAL. WHAT SAY WE TEAM UP?

9-2

JIM DAVIS

© 1981 United Feature Syndicate, Inc.

MAYBE I COULD BE AS POPULAR AS NERMAL IF I LEARNED TO DANCE

JIM DAVIS

9-3

I THINK I HURT SOMETHING

© 1981 United Feature Syndicate, Inc.

SWIPE!

I HATE
MONDAYS

© 1981 United Feature Syndicate, Inc.

HEE
HEE

HA HA HA!

WHEN YOU'RE BUILT
LOW TO THE GROUND,
A WALK IN THE GRASS
CAN BE TICKLISH

© 1981 United Feature Syndicate, Inc.

SURPRISE, GARFIELD! I GOT YOU A SCRATCHING POST

GEE, THANKS

9-11

SCRATCH
SCRATCH
SCRATCH

© 1981 United Feature Syndicate, Inc.

YAWN

© 1981 United Feature Syndicate, Inc.

JIM DAVIS   9-12

ARRRGH!

WHY ARE YOU WEARING MY READING GLASSES?

ALL THE BETTER TO SCARE YOU WITH, MY DEAR

RATS!

JIM DAVIS 9-13

© 1981 United Feature Syndicate, Inc.

I WENT AND DID IT AGAIN

HERE I AM, DOOMED TO DIE AGAIN. IF I STAY UP HERE I'LL STARVE. IF I JUMP I'LL BECOME A CAT PANCAKE. I HOPE SOMEONE RESCUES ME

STUCK UP THE TREE AGAIN, GARFIELD?

HELP! HELP!

RATS, I'D LIKE TO SLEEP IN THIS MORNING, BUT I'M HUNGRY TOO

JIM DAVIS   9-14

© 1981 United Feature Syndicate, Inc.

GO FETCH THE PAPER, ODIE

JIM DAVIS   9-15

© 1981 United Feature Syndicate, Inc.

IF CATS CAN RUN **UP** TREES, WHY CAN'T CATS RUN **DOWN** TREES AS WELL?

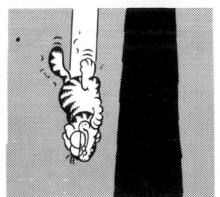

GARFIELD, YOU ARE VERY, VERY STUPID

9-18

OWNING A PET IS IDEAL FOR SINGLE PEOPLE. WE HAVE COMPANIONSHIP WITHOUT THE HASSLE OF RAISING A FAMILY

JIM DAVIS   9-19

© 1981 United Feature Syndicate, Inc.

WIPE YOUR FEET BEFORE COMING INTO THE HOUSE!

OKAY, DAD

9-29

DIAL
DIAL
DIAL

HELLO, JOE'S GARAGE? CAN YOU LOOK AT MY CAR?

I'D LIKE TO BRING HIM IN FOR A CHECKUP

BUT I JUST HAD ONE

YOU'D BETTER FLUSH OUT HIS SYSTEM...

TIGHTEN HIS HOSES

REPLACE ALL THE WORN PARTS

OH YES, AND HAVE HIM REUPHOLSTERED

JIM DAVIS

GARFIELD?

ABU DHABI

10-4

© 1981 United Feature Syndicate, Inc.

RRRRR

I THOUGHT YOU ASKED ME TO DINNER

OLD HABITS ARE HARD TO BREAK

© 1981 United Feature Syndicate, Inc.

I LOVE THOSE POINTY LITTLE EARS OF YOURS AND THOSE LUSCIOUS RUBY RED LIPS

AND I LOVE LISTENING TO THE MELODIC STRAINS OF THE WIND WHISTLING THROUGH THE GAP BETWEEN YOUR FRONT TEETH

YOU WENT ONE TOO FAR, FELLA

YOU'RE CUTE WHEN YOU'RE ANGRY

© 1981 United Feature Syndicate, Inc.

HERE, CATCH, GARFIELD

GOOD BOY!

© 1981 United Feature Syndicate, Inc.

I THINK I HEAR THE PAPERBOY

NOW I'M GOING TO CATCH THE MORNING PAPER

STUPID WEEKEND EDITION

JIM DAVIS   10-11

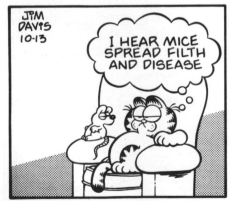

JIM DAVIS
10-21

PICK
PICK

PICK
PICK

WELL, WELL.
WHAT HAVE
WE HERE?

CALL IT A
NERVOUS
HABIT

PICK

JIM
DAVIS

SCRATCH
SCRATCH
SCRATCH

SCRATCH
SCRATCH

TIMBER

10-22

ONE STEP CLOSER AND I'LL PUT THAT TONGUE IN A SPLINT

YOU GOTTA SPEAK THEIR LANGUAGE

© 1981 United Feature Syndicate, Inc.

SOME PEOPLE SAY I'M MEAN, BUT THEY NEVER KNEW MY UNCLE NICK. HE USED TO EAT WHOLE CHICKENS

BUT UNCLE NICK WASN'T VERY BRIGHT. ONE DAY HE JUMPED AN OSTRICH BY MISTAKE

HIS LAST WORDS WERE: "THAT'S THE BIGGEST CHICKEN I EVER SAW"

© 1981 United Feature Syndicate, Inc.

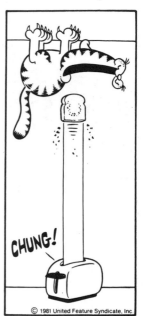

GARFIELD WILL BE IN HERE ANY MINUTE TO WAKE ME FOR BREAKFAST

11-8   JIM DAVIS

HE'LL PRY MY EYE OPEN TO SEE IF I'M AWAKE

© 1981 United Feature Syndicate, Inc.

THEN HE WILL TAP DANCE ON MY HEAD

AND THEN HE'LL SIT ON MY CHEST AND BREATHE IN MY FACE UNTIL I GET UP!

OKAY! OKAY!

WHAT DID I DO?

LOOK, GARFIELD. MOM MADE A SWEATER FOR YOU

JIM DAVIS 11-9

I'VE NEVER LIKED YOUR MOTHER

© 1981 United Feature Syndicate, Inc.

JIM DAVIS 11-10

© 1981 United Feature Syndicate, Inc.

11-11

11-12 © 1981 United Feature Syndicate, Inc.

WHAT'S SO SPECIAL ABOUT A PET-OWNER RELATIONSHIP, GARFIELD?

COULD IT BE EVERYONE NEEDS SOMEONE TO LORD OVER?

COULD BE

© 1981 United Feature Syndicate, Inc. JIM DAVIS

BUT WHAT DO YOU GET OUT OF IT?

11-13

YOU KNOW, GARFIELD...

© 1981 United Feature Syndicate, Inc.

JIM DAVIS

I WONDER WHAT PEOPLE WOULD DO WITHOUT CATS?

WITHER AWAY AND DIE, I SUSPECT

11-14

I WONDER WHAT CATS WOULD DO WITHOUT PEOPLE?

WHO'D CHANGE OUR KITTY LITTER?

HEH, HEH. JUST LOOK AT THAT. GARFIELD HAS HIS BED AND HIS FOOD. HE'S IN KITTY HEAVEN. CATS HAVE SUCH SIMPLE PLEASURES

JIM DAVIS 11-20

© 1981 United Feature Syndicate, Inc.

SPENDING AN ENTIRE WEEK IN BED WAS FUN

JIM DAVIS 11-21

BUT I CRAVE MORE VARIETY THAN THAT

© 1981 United Feature Syndicate, Inc.

NOW I THINK I'LL SPEND AN ENTIRE WEEK IN THIS EASY CHAIR

JIM DAVIS

11-22

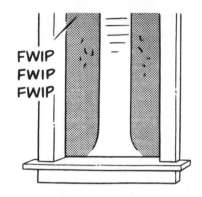

11-25

I'D CRY OUT
FOR HELP

BUT I COULDN'T
HANDLE THAT

PREDICAMENTS ARE
EMBARRASSING
ONLY WHEN NOTICED
BY SOMEONE ELSE

11-26

FOLD
FOLD

JIM DAVIS
12-2

CAN I PLAY TOO?

SURE...
GRAB
HOLD

© 1981 United Feature Syndicate, Inc.

SLEEP ON MY TEDDY BEAR, WILL YOU?!

Z

JIM DAVIS
12-3

Z

I WISH I COULD DO THAT

Z

© 1981 United Feature Syndicate, Inc.

WHAT ARE YOU DOING BACK IN BED, GARFIELD? IT'S NOT EVEN NOON YET

AS FAR AS I'M CONCERNED, THE DAY IS OVER

JIM DAVIS

12-6

TIME PASSES
SLOWLY ON
A WEEKEND

JIM
DAVIS

12-13

A FLY CRAWLS
UP THE WALL

© 1981 United Feature Syndicate, Inc

ONE OF THOSE
IRIDESCENT
FLYS OF FALL

TIME PASSES
SLOWLY ON
A WEEKEND

THAT'S MY JON.
HE'S RAISED
BOREDOM TO
AN ART FORM

12-14

© 1981 United Feature Syndicate, Inc.

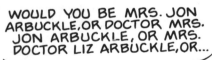

12-15   © 1981 United Feature Syndicate, Inc.

GOOD EVENING, LIZ. I HAVE A WONDERFUL TIME PLANNED FOR US

WE'LL HAVE DINNER, GO TO A MOVIE, AND MANY MORE THINGS TOO NUMEROUS TO MENTION

© 1981 United Feature Syndicate, Inc.

YOU BROUGHT THE CAT

THAT WAS ONE OF THE UNMENTIONABLES

THANK YOU FOR A LOVELY DATE, JON

JIM DAVIS

KISS

12-19

© 1981 United Feature Syndicate, Inc.

YAH TAH TAH TAH, YAH TAH TAH TAH

HUMAN LOVE... IT'S SO GLANDULAR

CLICK

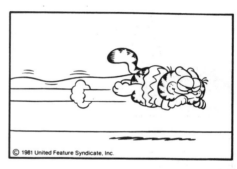

HA HA, AREN'T YOU CUTE! HERE, HAVE SOME FOOD

1-4-82

I HATE MYSELF WHEN I DO THAT

© 1982 United Feature Syndicate, Inc.

DID I EVER TELL YOU ABOUT MY WEIRD UNCLE ROY? HE HAD A SPECIES CHANGE OPERATION. HE HAD HIMSELF CHANGED TO A DOG

1-5-82

IT WAS TRAGIC

HE CHASED HIMSELF TO DEATH

© 1982 United Feature Syndicate, Inc.

Garfield Goes Globetrotting

The GARFIELD strip appears worldwide.

Here's GARFIELD in English...

Spanish...

French...

German...

Danish...